MY FIRST ENCYCLOPEDIA

An eye-catching series of information books designed to encourage young children to find out more about the world around them. Each one is carefully prepared by a subject specialist with the help of experienced writers and educational advisers.

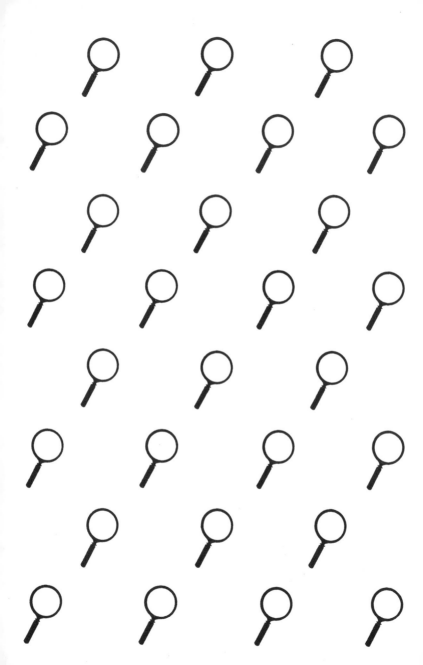

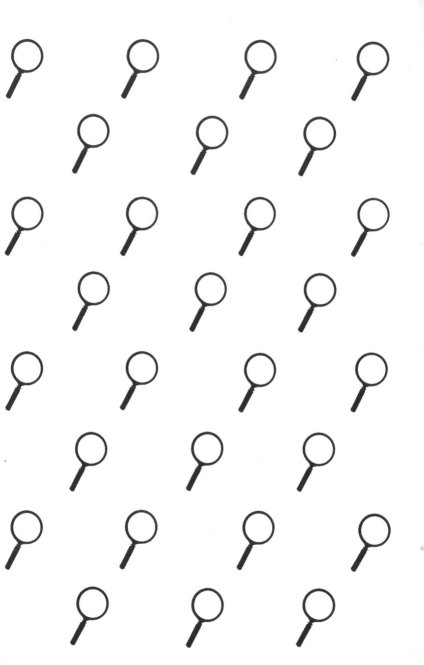

KINGFISHER
Kingfisher Publications Plc
New Penderel House, 283-288 High Holborn, London WC1V 7HZ

First published in paperback by Kingfisher Publications Plc 1994
2 4 6 8 10 9 7 5 3 1

1BP/0500/SF/(FR)/135MA

Originally published in hardback under the series title Young World
This edition © copyright Kingfisher Publications Plc 2000
Text & Illustrations © copyright Kingfisher Publications Plc 1992

ISBN 1 85697 269 0

Phototypeset by Waveney Typesetters, Norwich
Printed in China

MY FIRST ENCYCLOPEDIA

Science

Kingfisher

Author
Barbara Reseigh

Educational consultant
Daphne Ingram

Series consultant
Brian Williams

Editor
Camilla Hallinan

Designer
Brian Robertson

Illustrators:
Maggie Brand (pages 22-35, 54-55, 58-65, 74-75,
78-79, 85 & 106-109); Derek Brazell (80-81, 86-87,
93-95, 98 & 100-103); Bob Corley (19, 80-81, 86-87
& 113-116); Peter Dennis (38-41 & 44-51); Diane
Fawcett (90-91) Rebecca Hardy (91, 93-95, 97 & 99);
Nick Hawken (72-73, 79, 84, 92 & 99) Kay Hodges
(76-77) David Kearney (12-18, 92, 98 & 112) Pete
Kelly (42-43, 82-83 & 118-119) Tony Kenyon (20, 72
& 96-97) Stephen Player (110-111, 113-114 & 117)
Roger Stewart of Kevin Jones Associates (55-57,
70-71 & 106) Joanna Williams (68-69)

About this book

Ever since the first people were alive on the Earth, they have wondered about the world around them. What makes things move? Why do birds have wings? What is lightning made of? Where does an echo come from? How far away is the Sun? As you turn the pages of this book, you will find many of the answers to these fascinating questions.

Scientists have studied the world and used their ideas to improve the way we live. They have invented wheels, aeroplanes and electricity. They have saved many lives through studying medicine. Without the work of scientists, people would not have walked on the Moon or explored the deepest parts of the sea.

Science is one of the most exciting ways of finding out about what is going on all around you. It is not only about amazing facts but also about how to ask questions, investigate and test things out for yourself. Everyone can be a scientist, especially you! This books shows you how to start. Happy investigating!

CONTENTS

 BEING A SCIENTIST

WHAT ARE THINGS MADE OF?

ENERGY AT WORK

ELECTRICITY AND MAGNETS

WHAT MAKES THINGS MOVE?

♪ SOUND AND MUSIC

☀ LIGHT AND COLOUR

Being a scientist

What is science?

Science is all about finding out. It helps us make sense of our world. Science begins with observation.

That means looking at all kinds of things very carefully.

Sometimes we use our other senses to observe, too.

hearing

touch

smell

taste

microscope
magnifying glass

Scientists use special tools, such as microscopes, to help them observe. We can all be scientists. There is a lot left to find out about in the world!

$\wp$ Testing ideas

When we see things happening, we get curious and start to ask questions. We want to know what things are made of, what makes them work or why they move. There are lots of ways of finding out the answers.

When you see an aeroplane, you may wonder, "How does it stay up in the sky?"

You could start to find the answer by asking other people.

Or you could look at a book about planes and flight.

One of the most exciting ways of finding an answer is to test things out for yourself.

If you buy a packet of seeds, the instructions tell you to water the soil. What would happen if you didn't? Perhaps the seeds would grow more slowly, or not grow at all. You could do a test to find out.

The test must be fair. This means that everything must be the same in each tray: the same number of seeds, and the same amount of soil.

$\mathcal{P}$ Taking measurements

When scientists do experiments to test their
ideas, they take measurements to see what is
happening. They might measure size,
weight, temperature or number.

In your test, you
can look at how
many seedlings
appear. Count
them and write
down the results
every day. Then
you will have a
record of what has
happened.

WEEK 2	A	B
MONDAY	0	0
TUESDAY	0	1
WEDNESDAY	0	3
THURSDAY	0	6
FRIDAY		
SATURDAY		
SUNDAY		

Scientists use computers to help them record all the measurements they take. Then they can see how their experiment has turned out.

Tests do not always turn out as expected!

Check your chart. Has the test shown that your idea was right? Did any plants grow in the tray without water?

WEEK 2	A	B
MONDAY	0	0
TUESDAY	0	1
WEDNESDAY	0	3
THURSDAY	0	6
FRIDAY	0	6
SATURDAY	0	6
SUNDAY	0	6

Measuring time

Time is very important to scientists. They often need to measure exactly how long something takes. In the seed test, you measured how quickly the plants grew.

You could time a dripping tap. How many times does it drip in one minute?

Or you could time a friend skipping. How many skips does she do in one minute?

What would happen if you did these two time tests again?

The tap might drip the same number of times. But your friend might get tired and skip less. It's good to do tests several times, to see if the results are the same.

Over thousands of years people have invented many ways of measuring time.

A moving shadow on a sundial shows the time. A water clock has a hole, and as the water level drops, marks show how much time has passed. A candle measures time by burning wax away. Can you see how an hourglass measures time?

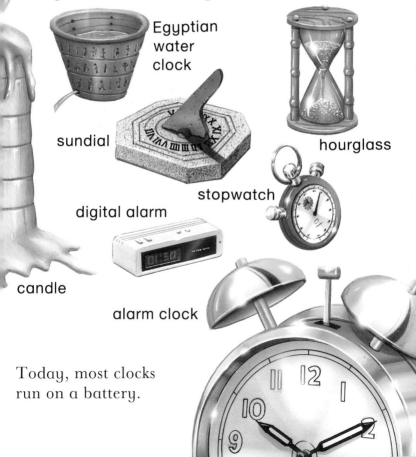

Egyptian water clock

sundial

hourglass

stopwatch

digital alarm

candle

alarm clock

Today, most clocks run on a battery.

Scientists at work

Scientists are always trying to find out more. They study different things and work in different ways. You can be a scientist too.

Astronomers use telescopes to study the stars.

Chemists study the substances that make up our world.

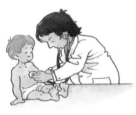

Doctors study medicine to keep people well.

Geologists study rocks to see what the Earth is made of.

$$A = \pi \times r^2$$

Mathematicians use special symbols to study numbers.

What are things

made of?

◊ Everyday materials

Have you ever thought about all the things around you? They are made of many materials. Some toys are made of metal, others of plastic. Some kitchen tools are made of glass, others of wood. Materials can be sorted in other ways too.

Look at these three groups of materials. One group is shiny. Another group is soft. And the third group is strong.

shiny

soft

strong

Can you think of other ways to group these things?

⬥ Building materials

steel and concrete skyscraper

Building materials have different jobs to do. Some are soft, so that they can be taken down easily.

cloth tent

Others are hard, so that the building will last a long time.

Many materials have to be very strong.

stone bridge

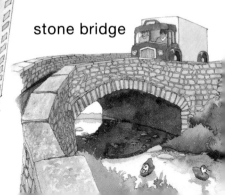

Some building materials have to stand up well to stormy weather.

Other materials have to keep the heat in and the cold out.

brick
lighthouse

glasshouse

tile roof

Most materials have to be waterproof.

Structures and 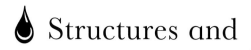 shapes

To make a structure strong, its shape is as important as the material it is made from.

Triangles have three sides. They hold their shape well and make a structure strong.

Can you find the triangles on this page?

Eiffel Tower

spider's web

coat hanger

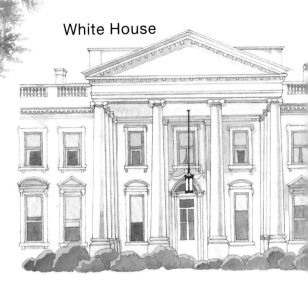
White House

Giant
Sequoia

tin
can

A cylinder is like a tube. It gives strong support.

Stone columns and tree trunks have a cylindrical shape, and they hold up a lot of weight.

Cylinders also make good containers.

27

🌢 Solids, liquids and gases

All materials are either solids, liquids or gases. Solids keep their own shape. They can be hard, like wood, or soft, like bread.

Liquids take the shape of their container. If you pour a liquid, it will run. Some liquids are sticky and run more slowly.

Gases don't even stay in their container, unless it is completely sealed. If they escape, they spread out all over the room.

Materials can turn from solids to liquids and from liquids to gases. It often depends on the temperature. Water runs out of the tap as a liquid.

But if we make water cold enough, it freezes into a solid – ice.

If we warm ice, it melts back to water.

If we heat water until it boils, it turns into a gas – steam. We call this change evaporation.

If we let steam cool, it turns back into a liquid. We call this change condensation.

Changing materials

Many materials change when they are heated or cooled.

When a volcano erupts, hot lava flows down the side of the mountain as a liquid. Then as the lava cools, it turns into solid rock.

As a candle burns, the wax melts and goes runny. It drips down the side of the candle, cools and goes solid again.

So, like water, candle wax can change and then change back again. These changes are reversible.

Some things change when they are heated, but cannot go back to what they were.

A fried egg can't go back to being raw!

A baked cake can't go back to being a runny cake mixture.

If you leave milk for a long time, it goes lumpy and smelly. This takes a few days. It only takes a few minutes to fry an egg, and an hour or two to bake a cake. But these are all irreversible changes. We can't undo them.

💧 Mixing and dissolving

When we are in the kitchen cooking, we often mix things together. But not everything mixes in the same way. Some substances seem to disappear in water, while others don't mix at all.

Try stirring a spoonful of salt into a glass of cold water. Then try a spoonful of sugar, and then flour. Are the results of your test like those shown here?

Salt	Disappears. The water stays clear.
Sugar	Settles at the bottom. The water stays clear.
Flour	Mostly disappears. The water becomes cloudy.

The substances that seem to disappear have dissolved in the water. Things dissolve more easily in hot water, such as sugar in tea.

When something dissolves, does it really disappear? Dissolve some salt in water and taste it. The water is salty!

The salt is still there, and you can get it back. Leave a saucer of salty water in the sun. The water will slowly evaporate and leave the salt behind. Taste it to see!

Dissolving dirt

Cleaning often gets rid of dirt by mixing and dissolving. We can clean muddy boots by rinsing them with cold water. The water mixes with the mud and loosens it.

We wash dirty plates in warm, soapy water. The detergent helps to loosen food stains so that they dissolve more easily in the water.

Some stains won't dissolve in water, even with a detergent. They dissolve only in liquids called solvents. Oil paint doesn't dissolve in water. But it dissolves in turps or white spirit.

There are lots of different washing powders, and they all claim to be brilliant. Why not test them for yourself? Take two pieces of old cloth and give them both the same stain.

Wash one cloth in warm water with powder A, and the other with powder B. Does one powder dissolve more of the stain than the other?

Amazing facts

Long ago, scientists called alchemists tried to change ordinary metals into precious gold. But they never succeeded!

Diamond is the hardest solid in nature. It is sometimes used in cutting tools.

The Eiffel Tower in Paris is 300 metres high and is made of iron. When it was built in 1889, it was the tallest structure in the world. Today the record is held by a steel television mast in North Dakota, USA. It is over twice as tall, at 628 metres.

Water is the most common liquid. Three quarters of the Earth are covered in water. Two thirds of your body are water.

Did you know that some animals can measure? When bees build a honeycomb, they measure the thickness of each wall by leaning against it to see how much it bends.

Energy at work

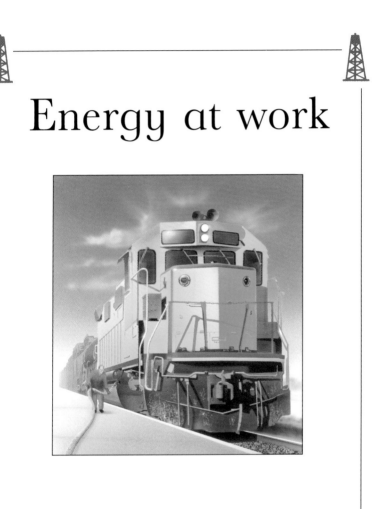

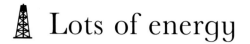 Lots of energy

We can't always see
energy, but we can see
its effects.

Energy makes things
go. A sailing boat
uses wind energy to
skim across the
water. You use
energy from the food
you eat.

There are many
forms of energy.

light

sound

heat

electricity

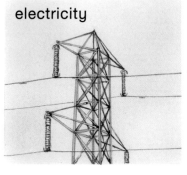

chemical energy – from food

chemical energy – from petrol

39

What gives us energy?

We get nearly all our energy from the Sun.

For instance, grass uses the Sun's energy to grow. Cows eat grass, and this gives them energy to produce milk. We drink the milk, and this gives us energy to live and grow.

Millions of years ago, long before there were
any humans, plants and animals were using
the Sun's energy. When they died, their
remains slowly turned into oil. We drill for
oil and turn it into petrol and diesel for cars.
So a car runs on the Sun's energy.

41

 Changing energy

Energy cannot be made or destroyed. But it can change from one form to another.

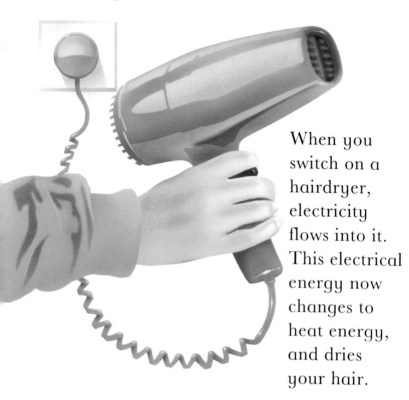

When you switch on a hairdryer, electricity flows into it. This electrical energy now changes to heat energy, and dries your hair.

At the same time, some electricity changes into movement and sound. The parts in the hairdryer are moving, and making a noise.

Many trains run on diesel fuel. Diesel comes from oil and is a source of chemical energy. To make the train go, the chemical energy changes into movement. Some of the energy changes into heat and sound.

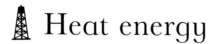 Heat energy

When you hold a mug of hot cocoa, it warms your hands up. But holding a snowball makes your hands go very cold.

This is because hot things pass heat to their surroundings, and lose some heat themselves. Heat always moves from warmer to colder things – from the mug to your hands, or from your hands to the snowball.

When heat energy is given or taken away, it causes a change in temperature. We can tell how hot something is by measuring its temperature with a thermometer.

Meteorologists are scientists who study the weather. They send thermometers up in balloons to measure air temperature high above the Earth.

Thermometers also measure the temperature of fridges and swimming pools.

We use a thermometer to take our body temperature. Our normal temperature is about 37 degrees Celsius.

45

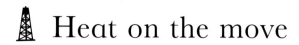 Heat on the move

Heat energy can move in different ways.
When two things are touching each other,
heat moves between them by conduction.
This is how a saucepan is heated.
A radiator heats a room by convection. It
warms the air next to it, and the air rises.

Cooler air replaces the warm air. Then this
air warms and rises. Now there is a stream of
moving air called a convection current.

Heat also moves by radiation. Hot things give off rays of heat. The Sun gives off rays of heat that travel through Space and keep us warm. So the Sun is heating the Earth by radiation.

Some materials conduct heat better than others. To test this, ask an adult to fill a glass with hot water. Put in a wooden spoon, a metal spoon and a plastic spoon. After a few moments, touch each spoon. Which material conducts the heat best and gets hottest?

Bigger and smaller

When materials get hotter, they get bigger. This is called expansion. When air is heated, it expands and gets lighter. A hot-air balloon flies because it is lighter than the cool air around it. When materials get colder, they get smaller, or contract. Over-head power cables contract and tighten in winter.

Water is unusual – it gets bigger as it gets colder and freezes. That is why water pipes sometimes burst in winter. Expanding ice cracks the pipe, and when the ice melts, water spurts out.

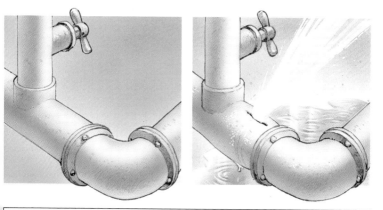

To see how water expands, fill a small, narrow-necked plastic bottle to the brim with water. Press a strip of foil on top, and put the bottle in the freezer. When the water has frozen, you will see that the ice has expanded and pushed up the bottle top.

 # Saving energy

Most of the energy we use comes from coal, oil or gas. These fuels are called fossil fuels, and they have stored energy from the Sun for millions of years.

oil   gas   co

We get fossil fuels from under the ground, but eventually the Earth's supply will run out. And there is another problem. When we burn fossil fuels in cars and power stations, they give off gases that pollute the air.

We must do everything we can to save energy, so that fuels last longer and there is less pollution. We can all help to do this.

We can switch off lights when they are not needed. A shower uses less hot water than a bath. We can stop wasting heat, by closing windows and insulating homes. And we can recycle our rubbish, not throw it away.

insulation

Amazing facts

The Earth is 150 million kilometres away from the Sun. The Sun's rays take just over eight minutes to reach us. Scientists think the Sun will go on making energy for another 5,000 million years.

Dr Frederick Sachs, an American scientist, made the world's tiniest thermometer. It can measure the temperature of single living cells, and its tip is 50 times thinner than a human hair.

Geologists think that there is enough oil under the ground to last us about 40 years, enough gas for 55 years and enough coal for 200 years.

Aluminium can be recycled many times. Each recycled drinks can saves 95% of the energy needed to make a new can.

Electricity

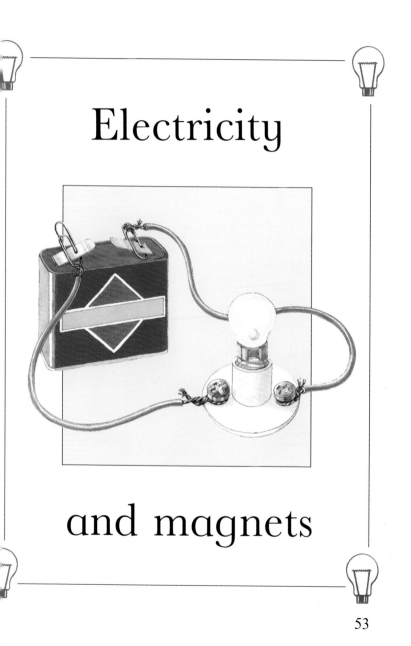

and magnets

Everyday electricity

Electricity is very important in our everyday world. Think of all the things that stop working if there is a power cut.

There are two sorts of electricity. One is called static electricity. It is made by rubbing materials together. You can rub things yourself to see the effects of static. What happens if you comb your hair hard?

Your hair crackles with static and sticks up. Or rub a balloon on your jumper and watch it stick to the wall afterwards.

Electricity that travels along wires is called current electricity. ***Warning!*** *Electricity could kill you. Never play with switches, wall sockets or anything that is plugged in.*

How is electricity made?

One way to make electricity is to use energy from moving water. Under a hydro-electric dam, rushing water turns huge wheels called turbines. They drive a machine called a generator, and this makes electricity. Using water power does not pollute the air.

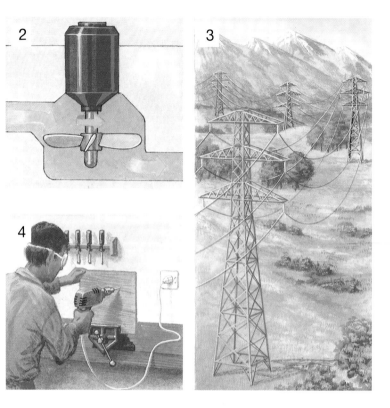

Other power stations burn coal or oil to turn
the turbines, or use nuclear energy.
Electricity is sent from the generator along
cables, which are buried under the ground or
hang from tall pylons. The cables bring
electricity to your home.

 # Batteries

Batteries store small amounts of electricity. They are useful because they are so easy to carry around.

Batteries contain chemicals. They provide electricity by changing chemical energy into electrical energy.

Warning! *Never take a battery apart – the chemicals inside are dangerous.*

Batteries make all sorts of things work.
So they are sold in many shapes and sizes.
Some batteries can be recharged so that they last longer.

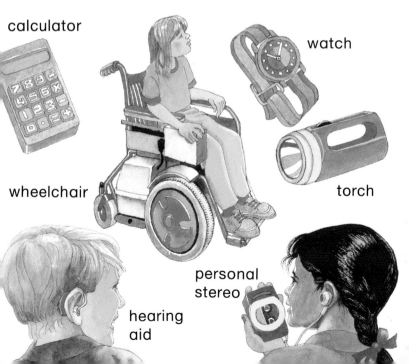

calculator

watch

wheelchair

torch

hearing
aid

personal
stereo

⚲ Circuits and switches

Electricity needs a pathway to flow around. We call this path a circuit. As long as the circuit is complete, electricity will flow.

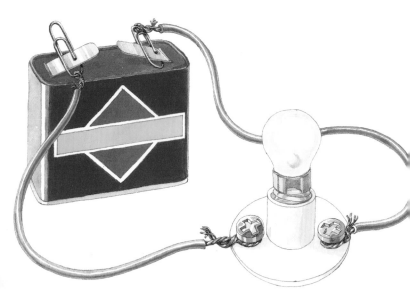

Electricity flows along a wire from one end, or terminal, of the battery. It passes through the bulb and lights it up. Then it travels back to the other battery terminal.

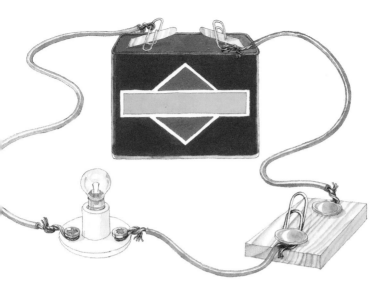

If there is a gap in the circuit, electricity cannot flow. A switch works by connecting the circuit to turn things on, and breaking the circuit to turn things off.

In this circuit, a paper clip is the switch. If it connects the circuit, the bulb lights up. If it breaks the circuit, the bulb goes out.

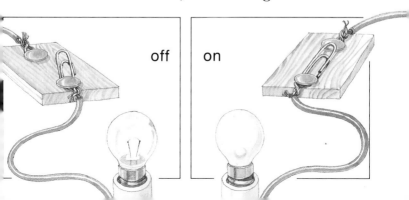

off   on

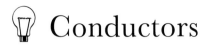 Conductors

Some materials let electricity flow through them easily. They are called conductors. Which of these objects do you think will conduct electricity from the battery?

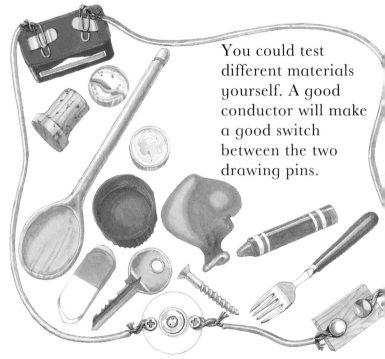

You could test different materials yourself. A good conductor will make a good switch between the two drawing pins.

Tall buildings have a lightning conductor. Lightning is powerful static electricity, but it flows safely down the metal strip.

Some materials don't let electricity flow through them. They are called insulators. Plastic, rubber and cloth are insulators.

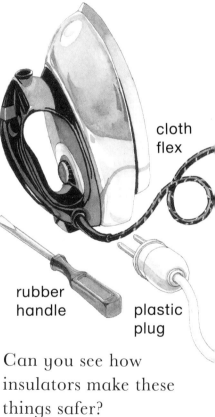

cloth flex

rubber handle

plastic plug

Can you see how insulators make these things safer?

63

💡 Magnets

Magnets pull some materials towards them. A magnet will pull or attract a paper clip, for example. But some materials are not magnetic and will not be attracted.

To find out which materials are magnetic, test things with a magnet. Does your magnet attract anything not made of metal?

Every magnet has two ends called poles – a north and a south pole. Close together, the north pole of one magnet will attract the south pole of the other. But two of the same poles will push apart!

The Earth is like a giant magnet. It has a magnetic north pole and a magnetic south pole. The poles of your magnet are attracted to the Earth's magnetic poles.

The needle inside a compass is a magnet. It swings round to show where north is.

You can make a compass by magnetizing a needle. Stroke the needle in the same direction about 50 times with one end of your magnet. Tape the needle to a flat cork and float it in water. The ends of your needle will point north and south!

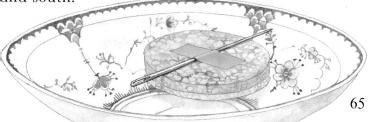

65

Amazing facts

The world's most powerful power station is the hydro-electric plant on the Paraná River in South America. It has the world's biggest dam.

Modern windmills called wind turbines produce electricity. To produce a lot of power, groups of turbines are placed together in "wind farms".

American scientist Benjamin Franklin (1706-1790) showed that lightning was electricity when he flew a kite in a thunderstorm. But the experiment was very dangerous and he was lucky to survive.

How do birds find their way when they migrate across thousands of miles? Scientists think their brain contains magnetic iron that acts like a compass.

What makes

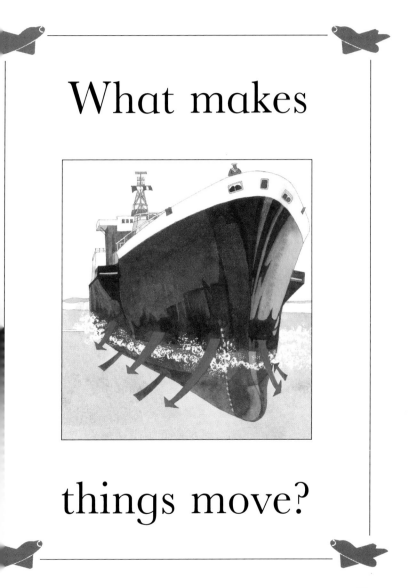

things move?

🐦 Pushes and pulls

Things move when something pushes or pulls them. These pushes and pulls are called forces. A force can make something start to move, speed up, slow down, change direction or stop moving.

An object will not move unless a force makes it move. Without forces, nothing would ever happen in the world. So when something does move, you know that a force is acting on it.

 How fast?

When a force makes something move, we can measure the speed. Speed is how far something moves in a certain time.

A Formula One car races along the track at about 380 kilometres per hour. A sprinter can run at about 40 kilometres per hour. A snail crawls along at about 0.02 kilometres (or five metres) per hour.

START

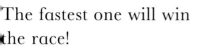

The fastest one will win
the race!

FINISH

You can work out speeds
by using a stopwatch.

Fastest human: Carl Lewis ran 100 metres in
9.86 seconds, in 1991.
Fastest animal: a peregrine falcon can fly at
350 kilometres per hour.
Fastest machine: the Helios B spacecraft can
travel at 252,800 kilometres per hour.

Opposite forces

When the canoeist pulls his paddle back through the water, this kayak is pushed forwards.

Every force has a balancing force that pushes in the opposite direction. So whenever anything moves, there is a balance of forces.

You need someone to balance you on a see-saw, to ride up and down.

load

Cranes make it easier to lift and move heavy objects on a building site.

This crane is lifting a steel girder. You can see that there is a heavy weight at the other end of the swinging arm, to balance the load. What do you think would happen if the weight wasn't there?

weight

🐦 Floating and sinking

Which things float on water? And which things sink? Make your own collection of objects and first guess whether they will float or sink. Then put them in water to see if you were right. An object floats because of balancing forces.

FLOATERS

SINKERS

The object's weight pulls it down, but water pushes back up on it. If an object is light for its size, the water's push is greater and the object floats. If an object is heavy for its size, its own push is greater and it sinks.

A lump of modelling clay sinks. If you make it into a boat shape, it floats! This is because the new shape is wider and flatter, so more water pushes back and holds it up.

That is why ships float – there is a lot for the water to push against.

Gravity and weight

The Earth pulls everything towards its centre, including us! This force is called gravity. It is the reason that things fall down and not up. You can throw a ball high in the air, but it will always fall back to the ground.

The Earth's gravity pulls on the Moon too, and keeps it circling around the Earth. But in Space there is so little gravity that things just float around, including astronauts.

The weight of any object depends on gravity. Scales measure the pull of the Earth's gravity on an object. We call this pull its weight.

The Moon's gravity is much less than the Earth's gravity. So a baby weighing six kilograms at home would weigh only one kilogram on the Moon!

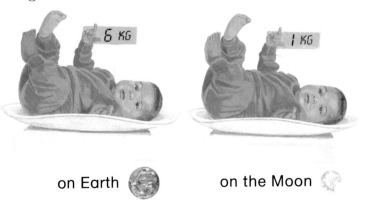

on Earth   on the Moon

✈ Pressure

When you walk on snow, you make deep footprints. But with snowshoes on, you make shallower prints Why?

The amount of force pushing on an area is called pressure. With snowshoes on, the pressure is less because your weight is spread out over a larger area.

Squeeze air out of a plastic bottle or tube. Let go, and the bottle regains its shape because air pressure forces air back into the bottle. But if you put the lid on before you let go, no air can get in. So the bottle stays squeezed.

When tyres are pumped up, air is squashed inside. This makes lots of pressure. So the tyres can support a truck which is carrying a heavy load.

✈ Sticking and slipping

Have you ever slipped on a wet floor? If so, you slipped because there wasn't enough friction. Friction is a force that tries to stop things sliding over each other. A bath mat increases friction and stops you slipping.

That is because rough surfaces produce more friction than smooth surfaces do.

More friction more grip

Water is slippery. When you ride on a toboggan, the pressure melts a thin layer of snow underneath. This makes the toboggan slide more smoothly and quickly.

We put oil in a car's engine so that its parts run more smoothly. Friction causes heat – rub your hands together hard to feel this for yourself. So oil also prevents the engine getting too hot.

Moving through the air

Moving through the air causes friction.
Because of the parachute's wide shape, lots
of air pushes against it.
So the parachutist
falls slowly and
lands safely.

In the same way, the
flying lemur uses wide
flaps of skin to glide
through the air.

Less friction will help a car use less petrol.
Coloured smoke in a wind tunnel shows how
the car's streamlined shape helps airflow.
Fish are streamlined for smooth swimming,
and cyclists for speed!

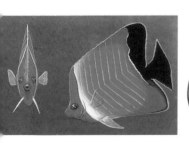

🛩 Flying things

What do a lot of flying things have in common? Wings! Have a look at the wings on this aeroplane.

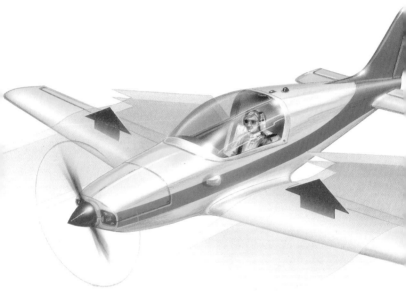

Air flows faster over the curved top of the wings than under the flatter bottom. The slower air has greater pressure, and this lifts the plane upwards.

The plane has a smooth streamlined shape. This lets air flow easily over a plane's surface. It cuts down the drag caused by friction as the plane flies through the air.

Birds have a similar, streamlined shape. And their feathers grow close together to make a smooth surface.

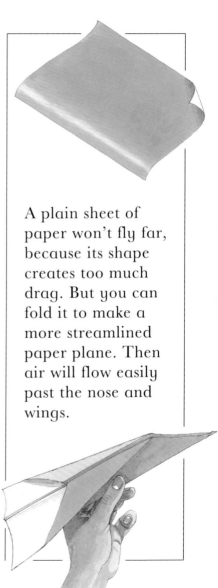

A plain sheet of paper won't fly far, because its shape creates too much drag. But you can fold it to make a more streamlined paper plane. Then air will flow easily past the nose and wings.

🐦 Machines for moving

Simple machines can make moving things easier. For instance, rollers and wheels help to reduce friction.

The monument of Stonehenge was built about 3,800 years ago. Its massive stones were probably pulled on rollers made of tree trunks.

Levers are simple machines that help us lift heavy weights. A lever is a bar that swings on a fixed point, like a see-saw. Your arm is a kind of lever. So is a crowbar.

When the Egyptians built their huge pyramids, they must have moved the heavy blocks of stone with wooden levers.

A wheelbarrow is a lever and a wheel combined.

Amazing facts

There is hardly any gravity in Space. Without Earth's gravity to weigh them down, astronauts grow a bit taller in Space.

Leonardo da Vinci (1452-1519) was a famous painter. But he was also a scientist, and he drew plans of helicopters and parachutes. His notebooks are hard to read, because he used mirror writing. He was afraid people would steal his ideas.

The official airspeed record for a plane is 3,529 kilometres per hour, flown in a Lockheed Blackbird in 1976.

The world's largest flying paper plane was built in 1992 by school pupils in Virginia, USA. It had a wing span of over 9 metres and flew for 35 metres.

Sound and

music

♪ What is sound?

A sound is made by something vibrating – moving back and forth very quickly. As you speak, vibrations from your voice travel through air in sound waves.

To feel the vibrations, press a balloon to the front of a loudspeaker. If you turn the sound up, can you feel more vibrations?

You can't see sound, but you can see its effects. Put some rice on a home-made drum, and bang on a tin lid. Sound makes the rice bounce!

There is no sound in Space, because there is no air for sound waves to travel in. Astronauts talk to each other by radio.

Sound travels well through liquids and solids. Male sea lions bark loudly under water to keep other males away.

♪ The speed of sound

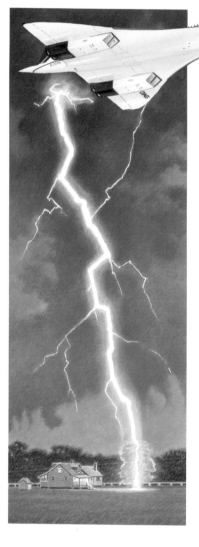

Sound travels through air at abou[t] 1,225 kilometres pe[r] hour.

Supersonic planes can fly faster than that. Concorde's to[p] speed is 2,333 kilometres per hour[.]

Lightning and thunder happen at the same time, but we see lightning before we hear thunder. This is because light travel[s] faster than sound.

Sound travels faster and further through water. A whale's song of roars, chirps and squawks can be heard by other whales up to 100 kilometres away.

To hear a sound through a solid, press your ear to a table and ask a friend to bang on a saucepan lid at the other end.

♪ How loud?

whisper: 20 decibels

talk: 60 decibels

heavy traffic: 80 decibels

pneumatic drill: 100 decibels

jet aircraft: 120 decibels

blue whale: 188 decibels

The loudness of sounds depends on the size of sound waves. Big waves sound loud.

We measure loudness in decibels. People whisper at about 20 decibels. But blue whales have been recorded singing at 188 decibels! No other animal is that loud!

Very loud noises damage our ears. So a road worker wears ear muffs to protect his ears from noise pollution.

noise pollution

Ears are well shaped for collecting sounds.
But not all ears are like ours!

95

♪ High and low

Some sounds are higher than others. A big double bass make low-pitched, booming sounds. A tin whistle makes high-pitched, piercing sounds.

The difference i in the sound waves. The more vibrations pe second, th higher th sound

Our ears can hear sounds between 20 and 20,000 vibrations per second. Compare this with other animals.

human
20-20,000

elephant
20-10,000

Sounds above 20,000 vibrations per second, or 20,000 hertz, are too high-pitched for humans to hear. We call these ultrasounds.

Doctors use ultrasound echoes to build up a picture of a baby in its mother's womb.

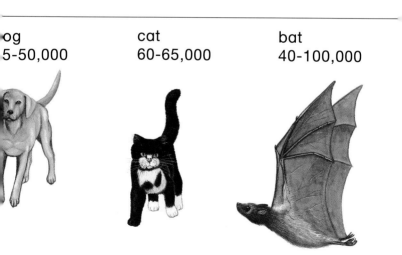

dog
5-50,000

cat
60-65,000

bat
40-100,000

♪ Echoes

When a sound bounces back to you, it makes an echo. This happens when sound waves hit a hard surface, such as a mountain side. Narrow spaces give the best echoes.

For an echo test, try shouting into an empty bucket. Your voice will bounce of the sides and sound louder.

Submarines and ships use echoes to see what is under the water.

This mini sub sends out sound waves, and measures the time taken for the echoes to bounce back. It finds a shipwreck below.

Swiftlets call out and use the echoes to find their way in the dark caves where they have nests.

♪ On the telephone

When you speak into a telephone, the sounds vibrate on the thin disc of a tiny transmitter. This changes the vibrations into electrical signals, which are sent along a wire.

When the signals reach yo[u] friend's phone, they vibrat[e] on another disc in a tiny receiver. This changes the[m] back into sounds.

Signals can travel from your friend's phone to yours at the same time, so you can hear each other's voice.
On a mobile phone, sounds are changed into radio waves and sent without wires.

You could make your own phone.

Find two empty, clean
yoghurt pots or paper cups.
Make a small hole in the base
of each pot. Thread the end
of a long piece of string
through each hole, and tie it
with a big strong knot.

Pull the pots
apart so that the
string is stretched
tight. Then speak
into your pot, while
your friend listens
with the other pot.
The sound waves
travel along
the string!

♪ Making music

You can make some simple musical instruments and form your own band!

Bottle organ:
glass bottles of the
same shape and siz
two spoons,
water.

Harmonica:
comb,
paper.

Shaker:
2 yoghurt pots,
dried beans,
sticky tape,
cardboard tube.

Guitar:
baking tin,
elastic bands.

Trombone:
plastic hose pipe,
bucket of water.

Scraper:
plastic bottle
with ridges,
pencil.

Pan pipes:
plastic straws,
cardboard or paper,
sticky tape.

Amazing facts

♪ The loudest sound ever measured was made by the Saturn V space rocket. When it blasted off, scientists recorded a noise of 210 decibels.

♪ The first supersonic flight was made in 1947 by Captain Charles Yeager over California, USA, in a Bell XS-1 rocket plane. Travelling faster than sound is called "breaking the sound barrier".

♪ The longest known echo in any building is heard 15 seconds after a door is closed in the Mausoleum in Hamilton, Scotland.

♪ Alexander Graham Bell (1847-1922) was an American scientist, and he invented the telephone. His assistant was surprised when he suddenly heard Bell's voice say, "Mr Watson, come here. I want you." That was the very first phonecall.

Light and colour

☀ What is light?

Sunlight is a form of energy. It is made by the heat of the Sun. It travels through Space as light waves, at a speed of nearly 300,000 kilometres per second! (Nothing else travels that fast.)

At night there is no sunlight, and it is dark. Long ago, people used fire to give them light in the dark. Later they burned oil lamps and wax candles. Today our main source of artificial light is electricity.

Transparent materials such as glass let light pass right through. Translucent materials let some light through. But opaque materials do not let any light pass through.

Collect different materials and hold them up to the light. How well can you see through them?

☀ Colour

Sunlight seems to be colourless or white. But really it is made up of several colours mixed together. You can see these colours in a rainbow, when sunlight passes through raindrops and gets split up. The seven colours of a rainbow are red, orange, yellow, green, blue, indigo and violet.

Can you mix these colours back together, to get white?

Cut out a card disc and mark it into seven sections. Colour the sections with the rainbow colours. Put a pencil through the middle and spin the disc. What happens to the colours?

A prism splits light into different colours.

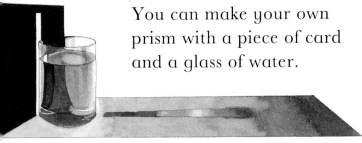

You can make your own prism with a piece of card and a glass of water.

Cut a slit in the card and stand it up against a window, with the glass of water in front of it. You'll see the colours more clearly if you have a sheet of white paper underneath.

Things are different colours because they soak up some colours and let others bounce off them. A banana lets yellow bounce off it and soaks up other colours. We see in full colour, but some animals see only in shades of black and white.

☀ Shadows

Light travels in straight lines. It can't go around objects. So if the object is opaque, it blocks the light and casts a shadow.

You can make shadow puppets with a torch in a dark room...

...and in sunshine.

The Earth spins right round once each day. So your outdoor shadow points in a different direction at different times. Also, your shadow is long in the early morning and late afternoon, when the Sun is low. At midday, the Sun is high and your shadow is short.

If a friend marks your shadow at different times during the day, you can make your own human sundial.

A sundial is a clock. You tell the time by looking at the Sun's shadow on the dial.

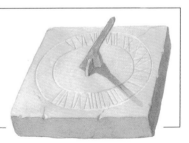

 Reflections

The Moon gives out no light of its own, but
sometimes we see it shining at night. This is
because light from the Sun bounces off the
Moon. Then we see the Moon, even though
we can't see the Sun! We might see this
"moonlight" reflected again on water.

When light hits any smooth, shiny surface, it bounces back and makes a reflection. When you look into a mirror, light bounces back at you and you see yourself.

Have you noticed that reflections are always back to front?

Mirrors are made of a sheet of glass in front of a thin piece of shiny metal.

Lots of other shiny surfaces reflect light.

Tricks of light

If you put a straw in a glass of water, it seems to bend at the surface of the water. This effect is called refraction.

Refraction is caused by light travelling at different speeds through different materials. It moves faster through air than through water. When it changes speed, it changes direction slightly too.

Put a coin in a glass of water and look at it from several angles. It seems to change shape and size, all because of refraction.

Refraction can make things look bigger, too. That's why a goldfish in a bowl seems to grow in size as it swims towards you!

The round goldfish bowl is made of curved glass, which can also bend light rays by refraction.

A magnifying glass is useful if we want to see things close up. The curved lens of glass increases the refraction.
So the coin looks bigger.

 # Lenses

Lenses are specially shaped to bend light. That's how they make things seem smaller and further away, or bigger and closer.

telesco

camera

binoculars

convex

Convex lenses curve outwards, and they can bend light to make things seem bigger. Concave lenses curve inwards and make things seem smaller.

concave

116

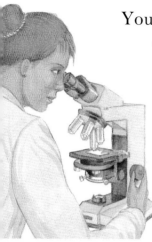

You can photograph things in close up with a zoom lens. You can look at faraway birds through binoculars. You can see distant stars with a telescope. A microscope makes things that are too small to see with your eyes look thousands of times bigger.

microscope

If you cannot see as well as you should, you might wear spectacles or contact lenses.

Shortsighted people cannot see faraway objects clearly, so they need concave lenses. Farsighted people cannot see nearby objects clearly, so they need convex lenses.

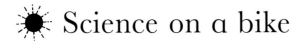

☀ Science on a bike

Your bike is full of science! It works well because it uses many of the ideas we have looked at.

The **wheels** are efficient machines. Their tyres have tread to grip the road with extra **friction**. You pump the tyres to keep up the **air pressure**.

The frame is made of strong metal, with two strong **triangle** shapes.

You use oil to prevent **friction**, so that the bike' parts run more smoothly.

You use **energy** to make **movement**. You do this by **pushing** down on the pedals.

Your helmet is **streamlined**, so that air doesn't hold you back.

You ring the bell to make a warning **sound**.

The bicycle lamp works on a **battery**.

A speedometer tells you **how fast** you are going.

When you want to stop, you pull a **lever**, and your brakes use **friction** to slow down the wheels.

What a scientific ride!

Amazing facts

Sir Isaac Newton (1642-1727) was one o the greatest scientists of all time. He used a glass prism to prove that light is made up of different colours. It is said that he decided to study gravity after seeing an apple fall from a tree.

The seven colours of the rainbow can be mixed together to make as many shades as you can think of. Scientists believe the human eye can see 10 million different colours.

In 1990 the Hubble space telescope was launched into Space to help scientists see further than ever before. Unfortunately it sent back blurred pictures. So in 1993 astronauts went up into Space and repaired the lenses.

INDEX

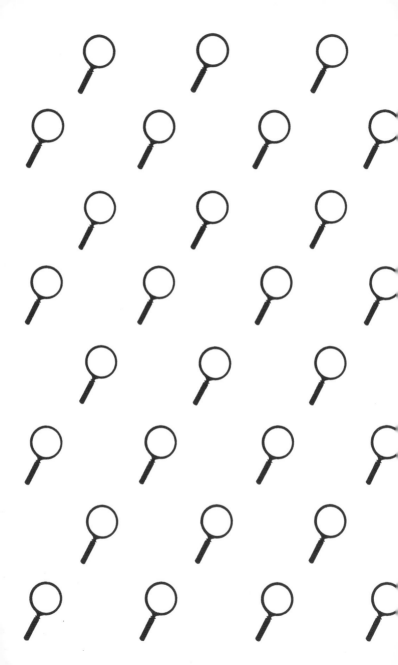

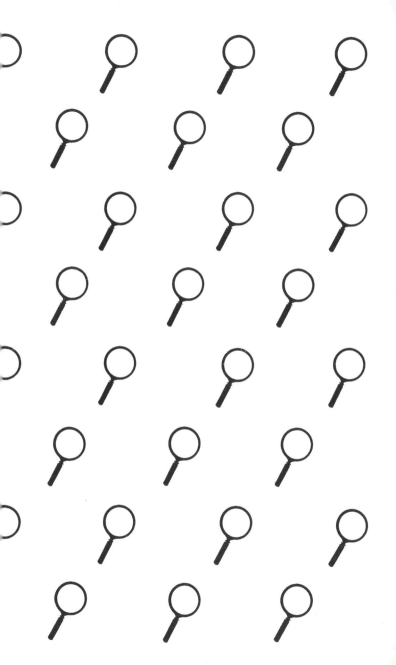